Y0-CZC-934

This book would not have been made possible without Petey. Thanks Petey! You were my furry best friend. Also, thank you Skip, Cheryl, and those of you who graciously read my rough drafts of this book. Nilah, you were a big help arranging some of the props and being Petey's princess. Erich, your volunteering to enhance the design of this book and reduce the printing costs has helped this book to become a more successful fundraiser. I appreciate all of your help. Ana Maria, thank you for all of your love and support. Danielle and Anthony, you were two very special young adults who bravely battled Leukemia and Lymphoma with strength, courage and determination. Sadly, you both left this earth much too early.

Lastly, another young person touched my heart. Her name is Braelynn and she is only three years of age. She was diagnosed with an inoperable tumor in her brain stem in June 2014. Currently, Braelynn is being treated at St. Louis Children's Hospital and St. Jude Children's Research Hospital in Memphis, TN. Knowing this precious and brave little girl is now battling this disease made me want to finish writing Petey's storybook, so Petey and I could send her some cheer. Thank you, Braelynn, for inspiring me to help children like you.

- Christine

For more infomation or to order more copies please email itsnotsoruff@aol.com

It's Not So RUFF Being a Working Dog!

Christine R. Salamone

Text copyright © 2014 by Christine R. Salamone

Pictures copyright © 2014 by Christine R. Salamone

Design by Christine R. Salamone

Layout by Erich J. Suellentrop

ISBN-13: 978-1500657147
ISBN-10: 150065714X

ALL RIGHTS RESERVED, EXCEPT AS PERMITTED UNDER THE U.S. COPYRIGHT ACT OF 1976. NO PART OF THIS BOOK MAY BE REPRODUCED, DISTRIBUTED, OR TRANSMITTED IN ANY FORM OR BY ANY MEANS. IN ADDITION, NO PART OF THIS BOOK SHALL BE STORED IN A DATABASE OR RETRIEVAL SYSTEM, WITHOUT THE PRIOR WRITTEN PERMISSION OF CHRISTINE R. SALAMONE.

Preface

This book was written as a tribute to my special dog Petey, AKC registered as "St. Peter the Pearly Gate Keeper." Petey was a black and red German Shepherd. Petey's mother, Serena, gave birth to him by cesarean section on April 29, 2001. At a young age, Petey enjoyed picking up items and carrying them in his mouth. He also was a large dog and loved being with me, and so I trained him to be my service dog. I have a neuro-muscular disease and needed his assistance. He helped me with my hands, arms, and legs by pulling my wheelchair, standing to brace me, carrying my items, and picking up items off of the floor. He always provided me with unconditional love whenever I needed it.

Petey knew he was not to be petted while working. However, there were a few times when he knew he was needed and actually allowed others to pet him. For example, one day we were with a lady whose grandmother had died. Petey sensed she was sad, so he went to her side and allowed her to use him for comfort by petting him. Another time, we saw a man we knew who was sobbing. I had known this man was at a very low point in his life. Interestingly, Petey always kept his distance from this man and never showed any interest in him. On this particular day, Petey left my side, positioned himself right next to this man, and allowed the man to hug him tightly and stroke his fur briskly. I was then able to seek help, so this man would be safe while Petey stayed with him willingly. Petey's instincts were confirmed later when I found out that the man had been planning to end his life.

When I volunteered for a hospice agency, I brought Petey with me. Even when he was working for me, Petey also knew when other people needed him. Sometimes patients needed to be cheered up or family members needed to be comforted. When he sensed someone needed him, he would carefully position himself next to the person and allow the person to pet him. As soon as the person stopped petting Petey, he would immediately refocus his attention back on me.

Petey was gentle, kind, friendly, sweet, loving, protective, funny, intelligent, and, most of all, patient. Sadly, in November 2012 Petey died suddenly and did not get to see his story written. Petey touched many lives while educating them about service animals and why they are important. They saw his commitment and dedication when he was working.

I want Petey's legacy to live on. I am donating all of the proceeds, exceeding the printing expenses, for each of these books to help individuals and their families battling with cancer and other childhood illnesses. Not only did Petey help many people, including myself, throughout his lifetime, but he also contributed to this book by posing for each of these pictures. May Petey's spirit now touch others who read his book and smile at his pictures. This is his story.

Once there was a black and red German Shepherd named Petey. He was a smart, kind, and loving friend who always liked to help.

Petey was trained to help a lady who had a physical illness. The nerves and muscles in her hands, arms, feet, and legs were weak at times.

She needed Petey to help pull her wheelchair, carry her bags, and stand to brace her to walk. Petey also liked helping other people.

Petey knew when people felt sad or alone. He helped the people feel better when he allowed them to pet and hug him.

He was always happy and willing to help wherever he was needed. It didn't matter if he had to work inside or outside.

Petey could always be heard saying, "It's not so RUFF being a working dog! A dog has to do what a dog has to do."

When a gardener is needed to help take care of the flowers, Petey is there. He quickly retrieves a hose and turns on the water because he likes to help.

Petey says, "It's not so RUFF being a working dog! A dog has to do what a dog has to do."

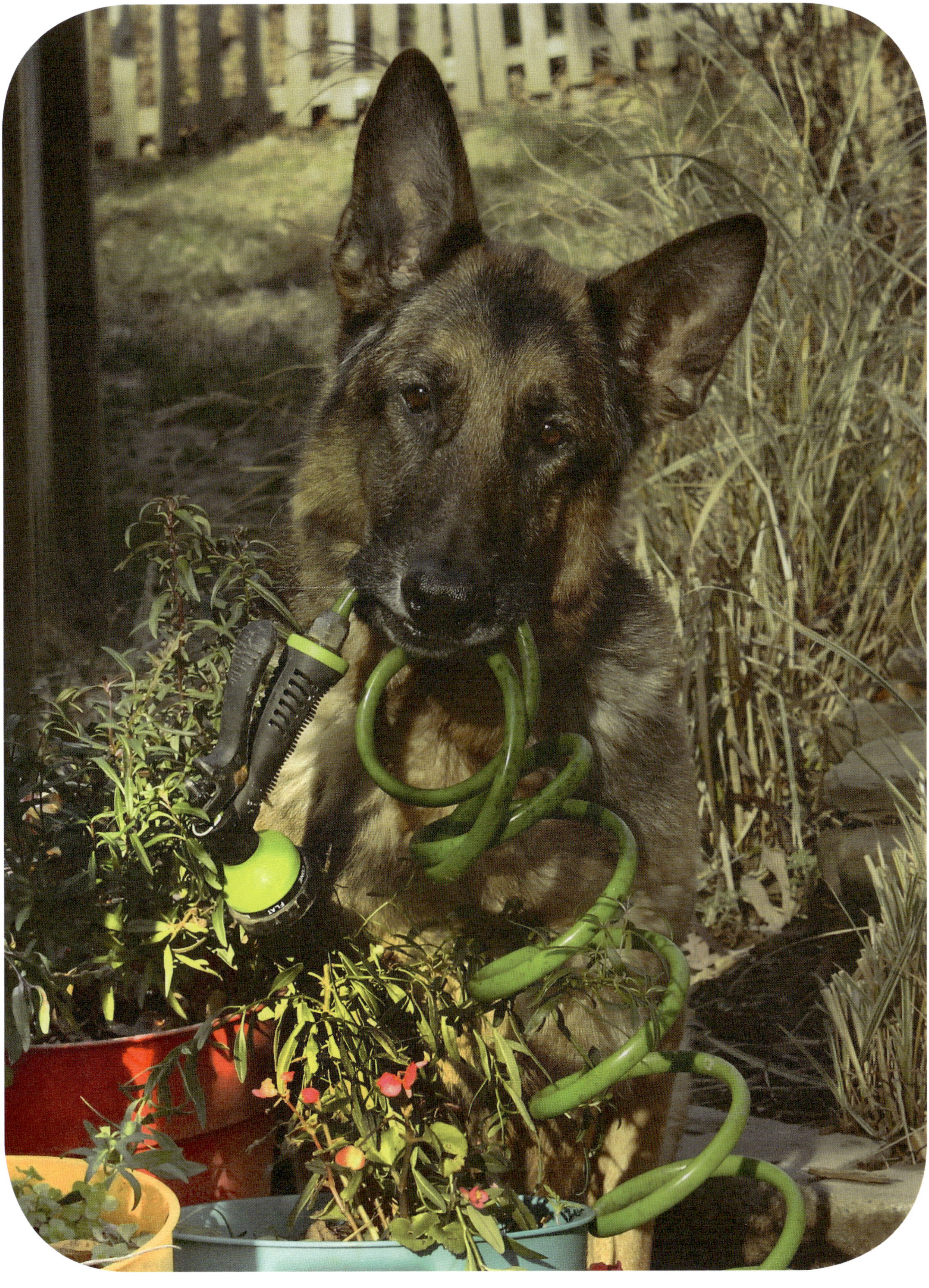

When a groundskeeper is needed to help with yard work, Petey is there. He quickly gets his rake and paper bag because he likes to help.

Petey says, "It's not so RUFF being a working dog! A dog has to do what a dog has to do."

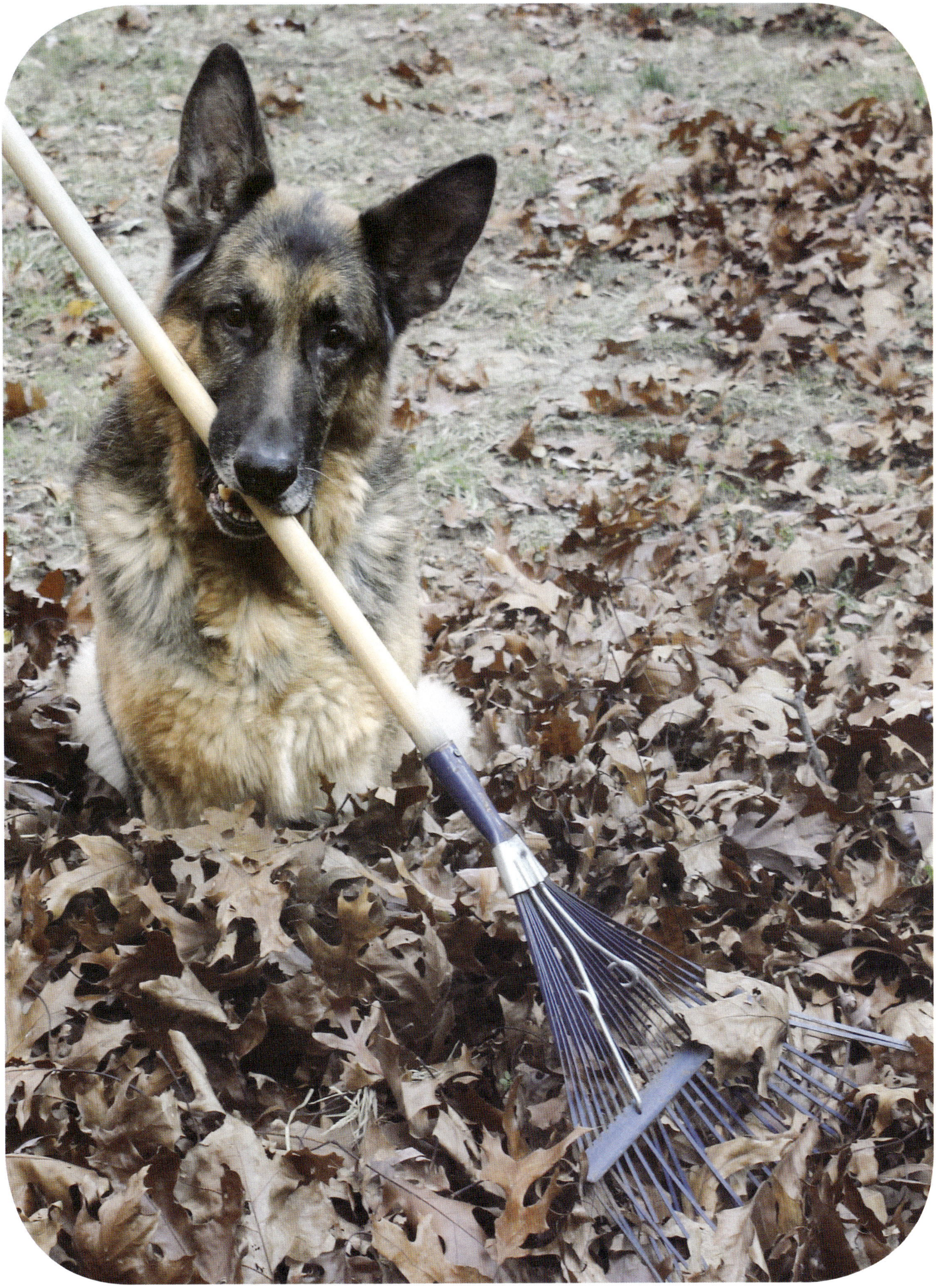

When someone is needed to help do the laundry, Petey is there. He quickly gathers a basket and the clothes because he likes to help.

Petey says, "It's not so RUFF being a working dog! A dog has to do what a dog has to do."

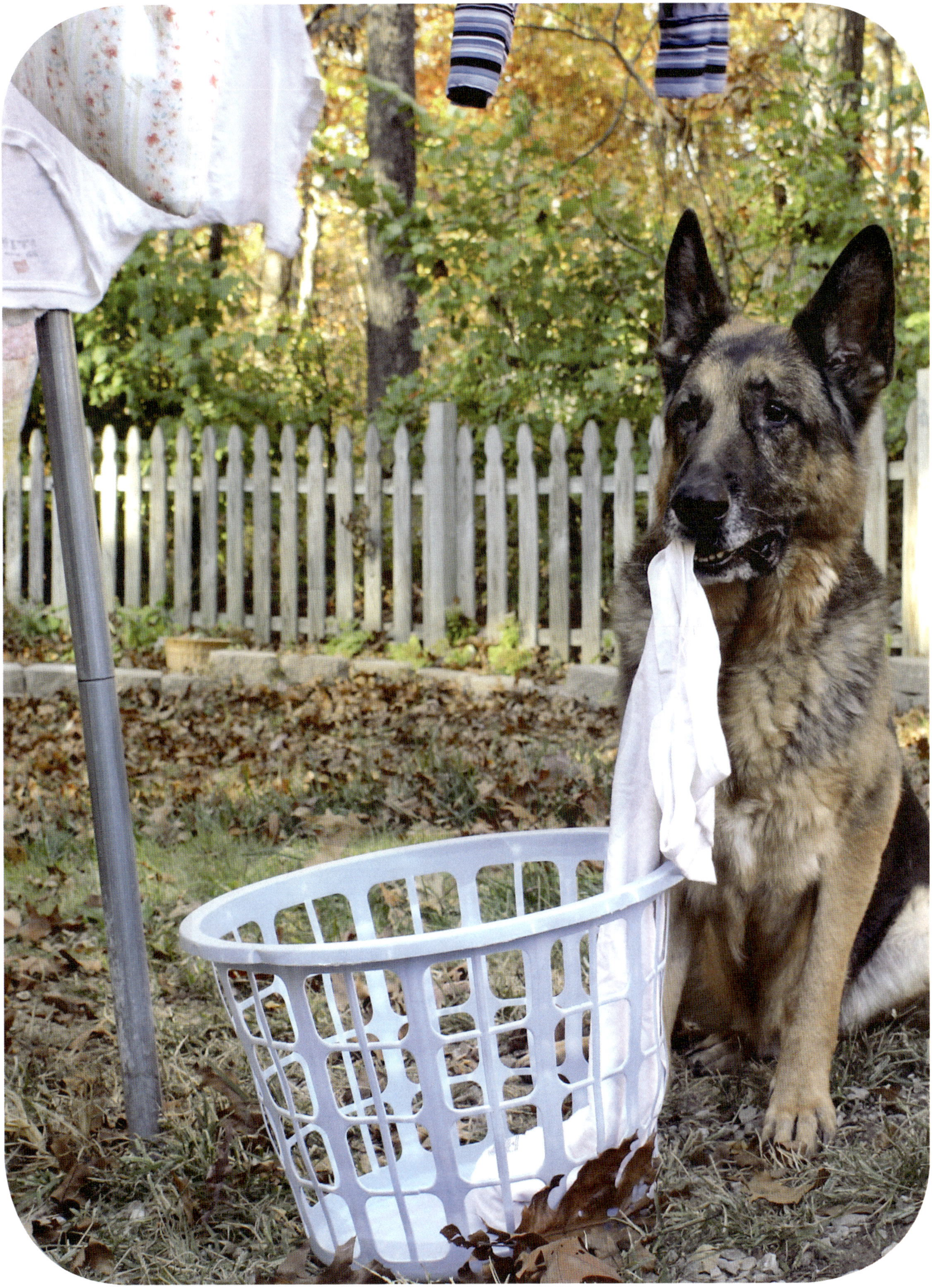

When a housekeeper is needed to help clean, Petey is there. He quickly fetches his broom and puts on his apron because he likes to help.

Petey says, "It's not so RUFF being a working dog! A dog has to do what a dog has to do."

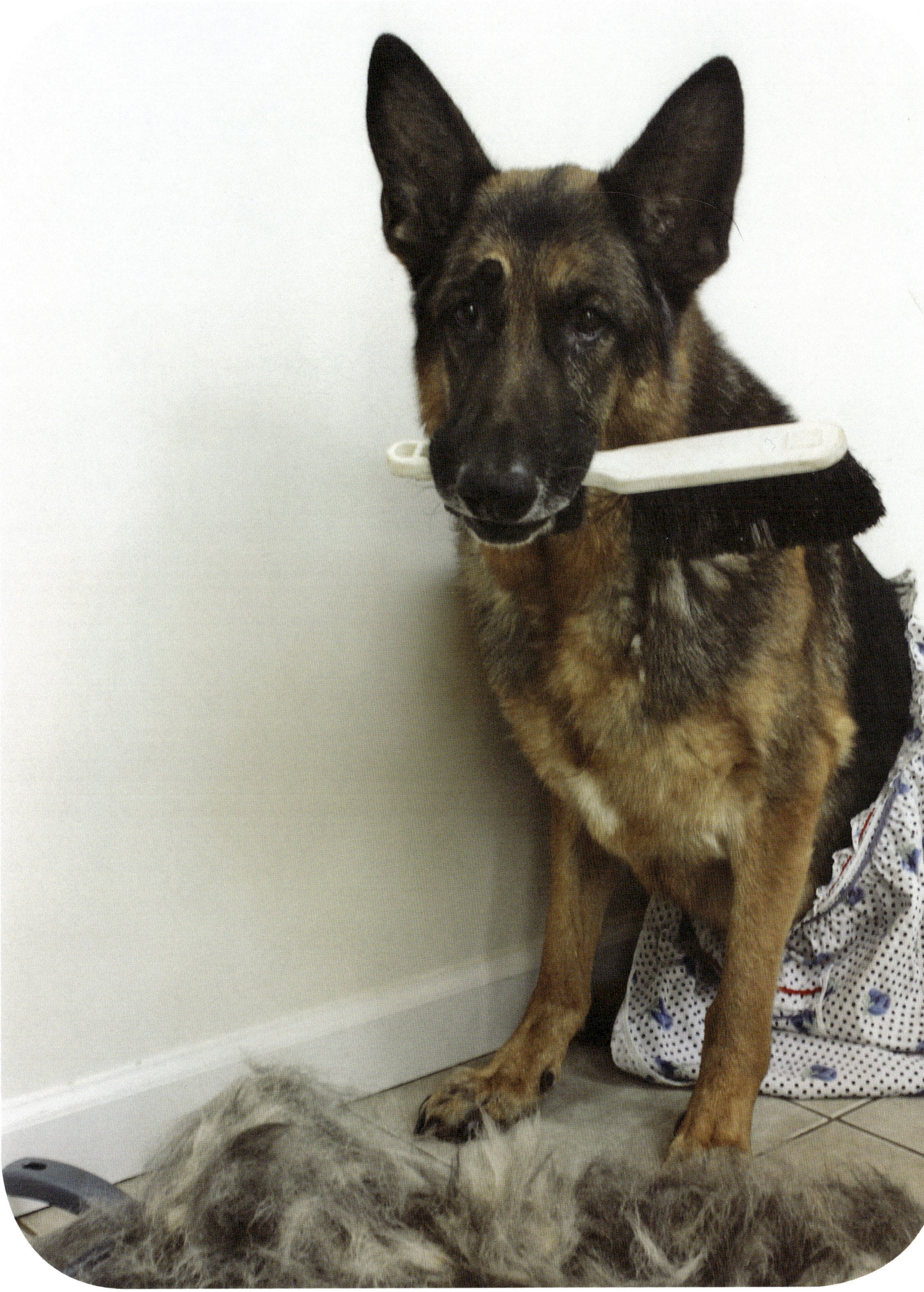

When someone is needed to help recycle and save the earth, Petey is there. He quickly collects paper and plastics because he likes to help.

Petey says, "It's not so RUFF being a working dog! A dog has to do what a dog has to do."

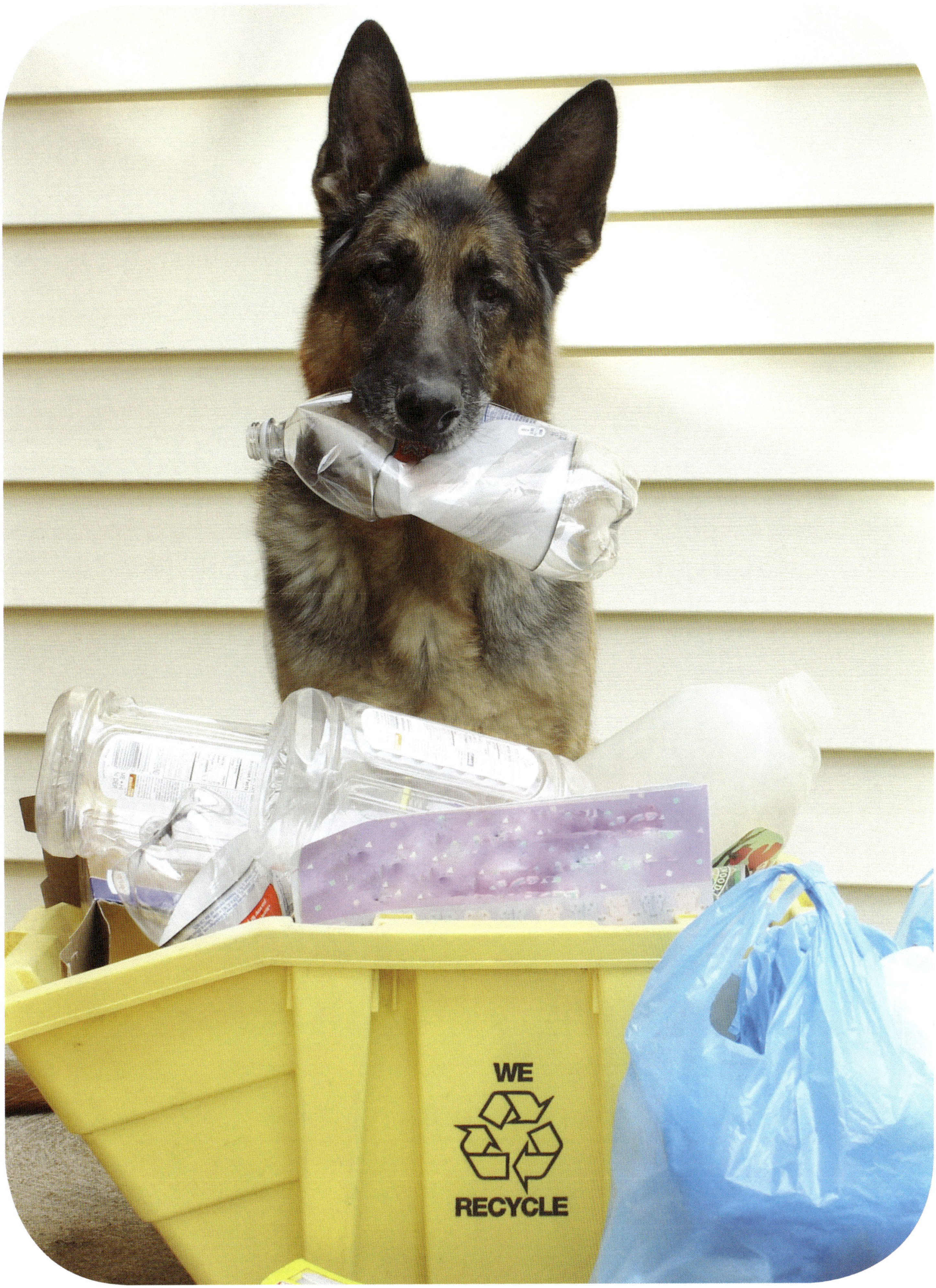
WE
RECYCLE

When a birdwatcher is needed to help watch the birds, Petey is there. He quickly retrieves his book and binoculars because he likes to help.

Petey says, "It's not so RUFF being a working dog! A dog has to do what a dog has to do."

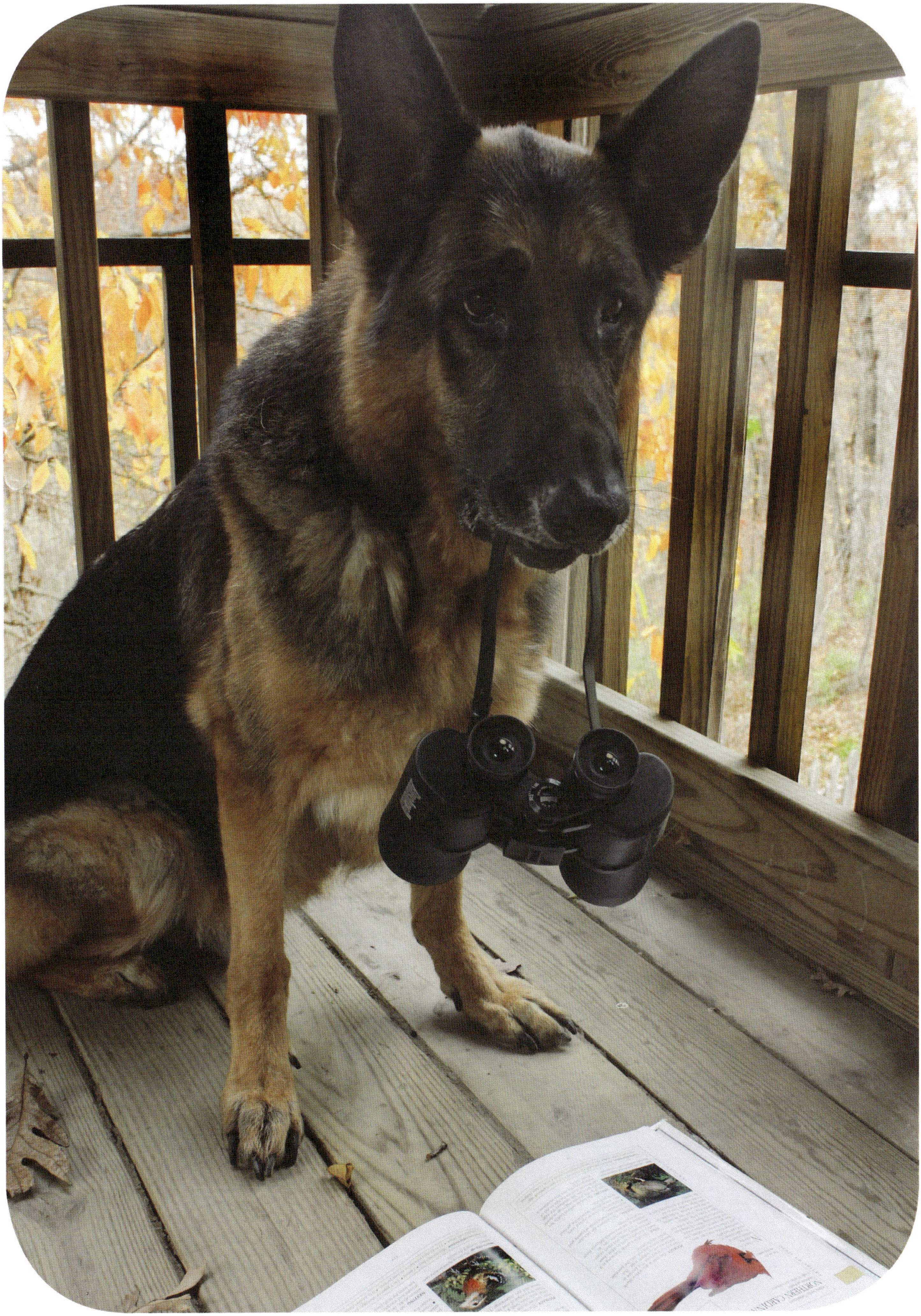

When a photographer is needed to help take pictures, Petey is there. He quickly grabs his camera and stand because he likes to help.

Petey says, "It's not so RUFF being a working dog! A dog has to do what a dog has to do."

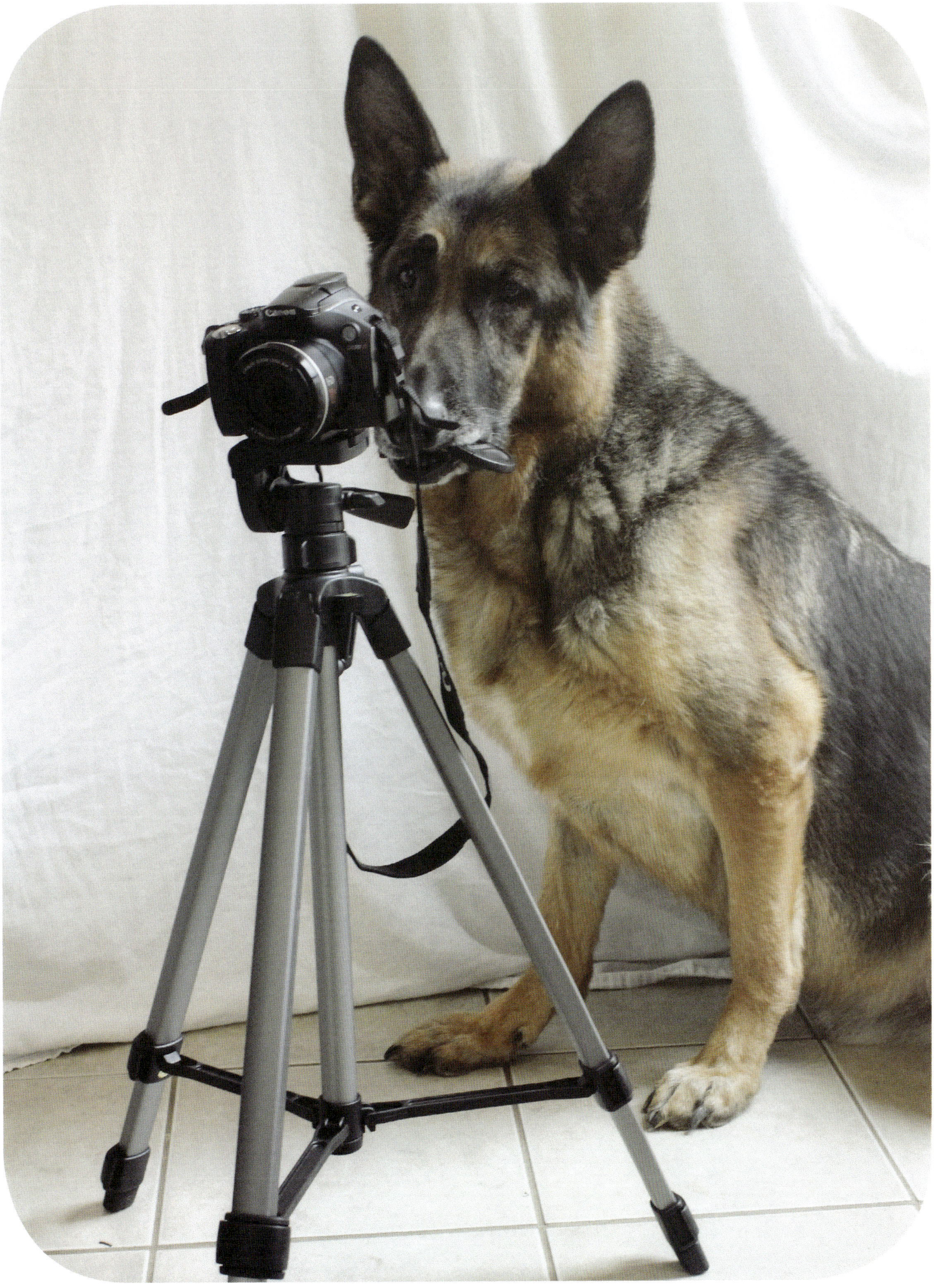

When a fisherman is needed to help catch the fish, Petey is there. He quickly hunts for his net and bucket because he likes to help.

Petey says, "It's not so RUFF being a working dog! A dog has to do what a dog has to do."

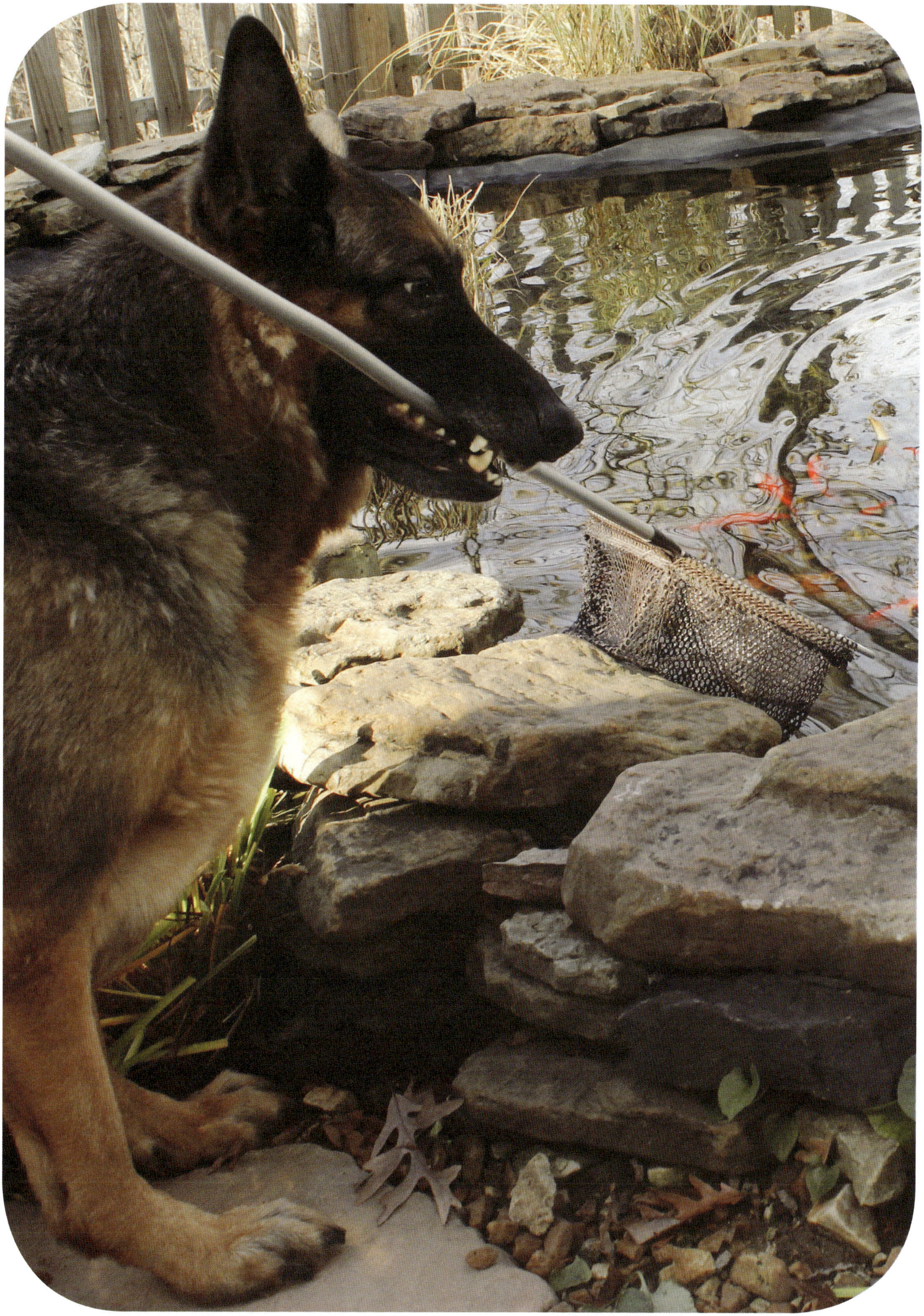

When a storyteller is needed to help tell a story, Petey is there. He quickly picks out a book and puts on his glasses because he likes to help.

Petey says, "It's not so RUFF being a working dog! A dog has to do what a dog has to do."

The German Shepherd Dog
GUIDE TO
A HAPPY HEALTHY PET
Liz Palika

When a student is needed to help with a school graduation, Petey is there. He quickly puts on his black cap and gown because he likes to help.

Petey says, "It's not so RUFF being a working dog! A dog has to do what a dog has to do."

St. Louis
Community
College
FLORISSANT VALLEY FOREST PARK MERAMEC WILDWOOD

When a teacher is needed to help children learn, Petey is there. He quickly retrieves his books and pens because he likes to help.

Petey says, "It's not so RUFF being a working dog! A dog has to do what a dog has to do."

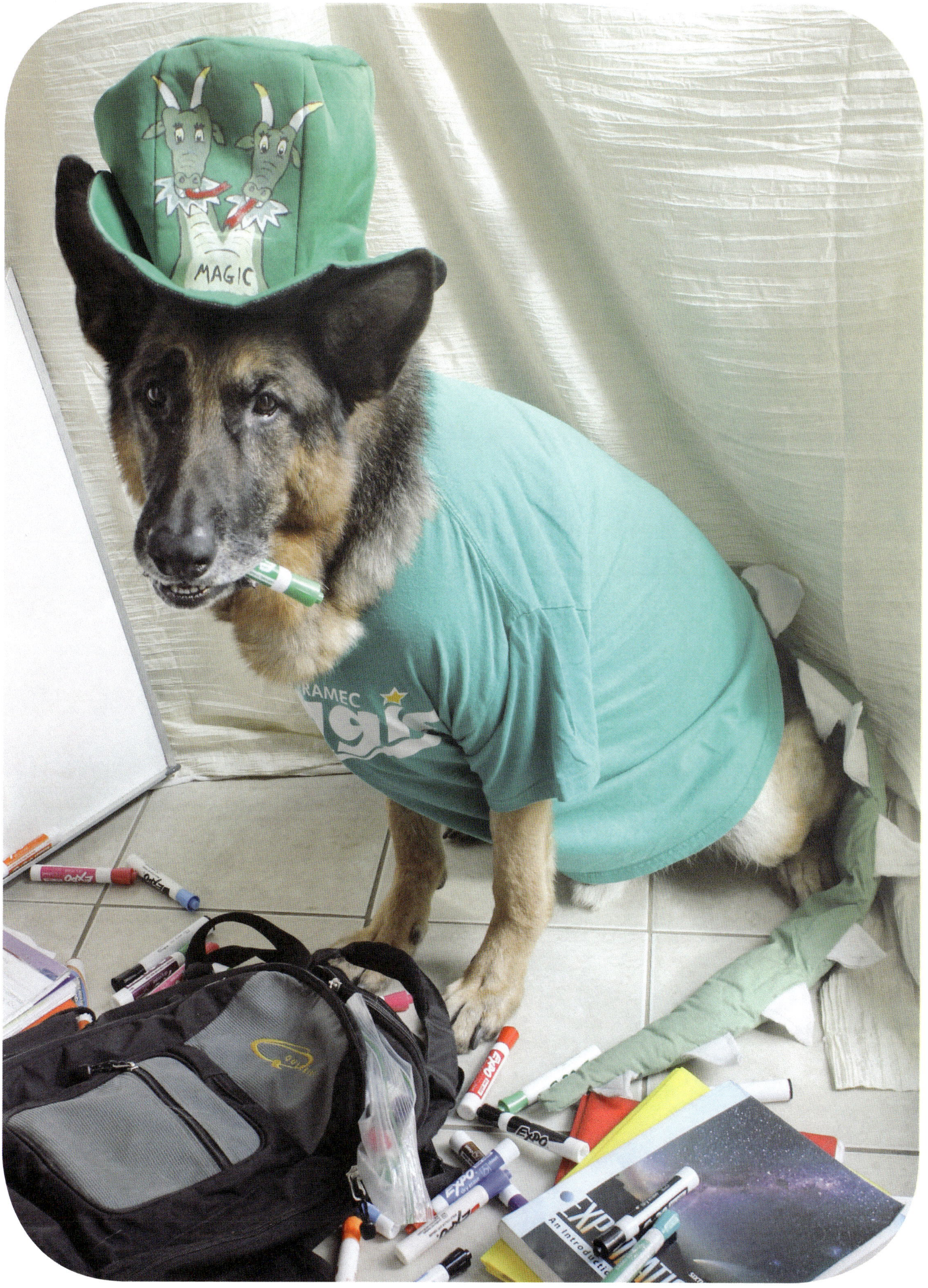
MAGIC

When a prince is needed to
help a princess, Petey
is there. He quickly dresses
up in his black top hat
and black and white
tuxedo because
he likes to help.

Petey says, "It's not so
RUFF being a working dog!
A dog has to do what
a dog has to do."

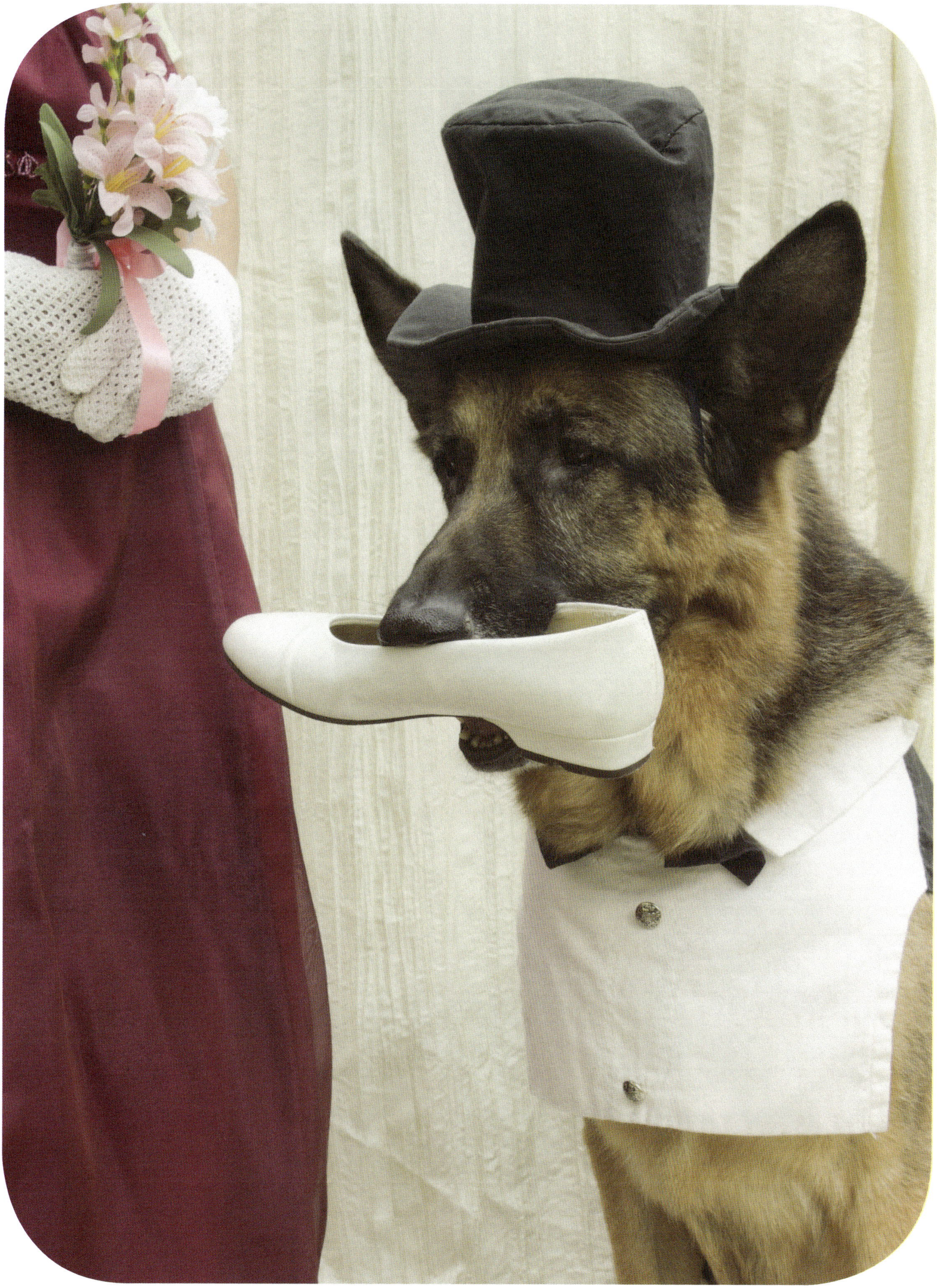

When a baseball player is needed to help the baseball team, Petey is there. He quickly puts on his hat and glove because he likes to help.

Petey says, "It's not so RUFF being a working dog! A dog has to do what a dog has to do."

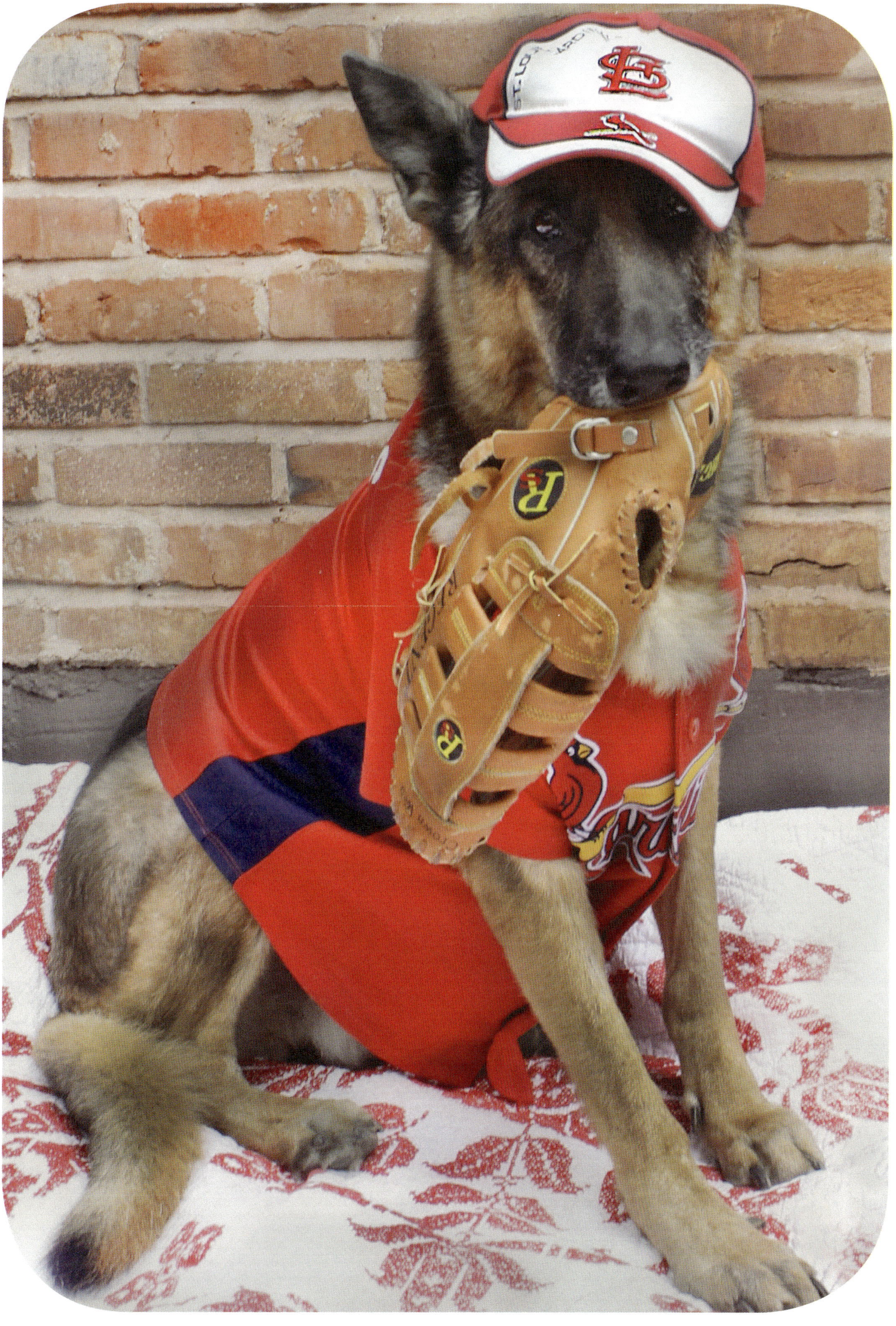

When a clown is needed to help in a circus, Petey is there. He quickly slips on his polka-dotted suit and rainbow colored wig because he likes to help.

Petey says, "It's not so RUFF being a working dog! A dog has to do what a dog has to do."

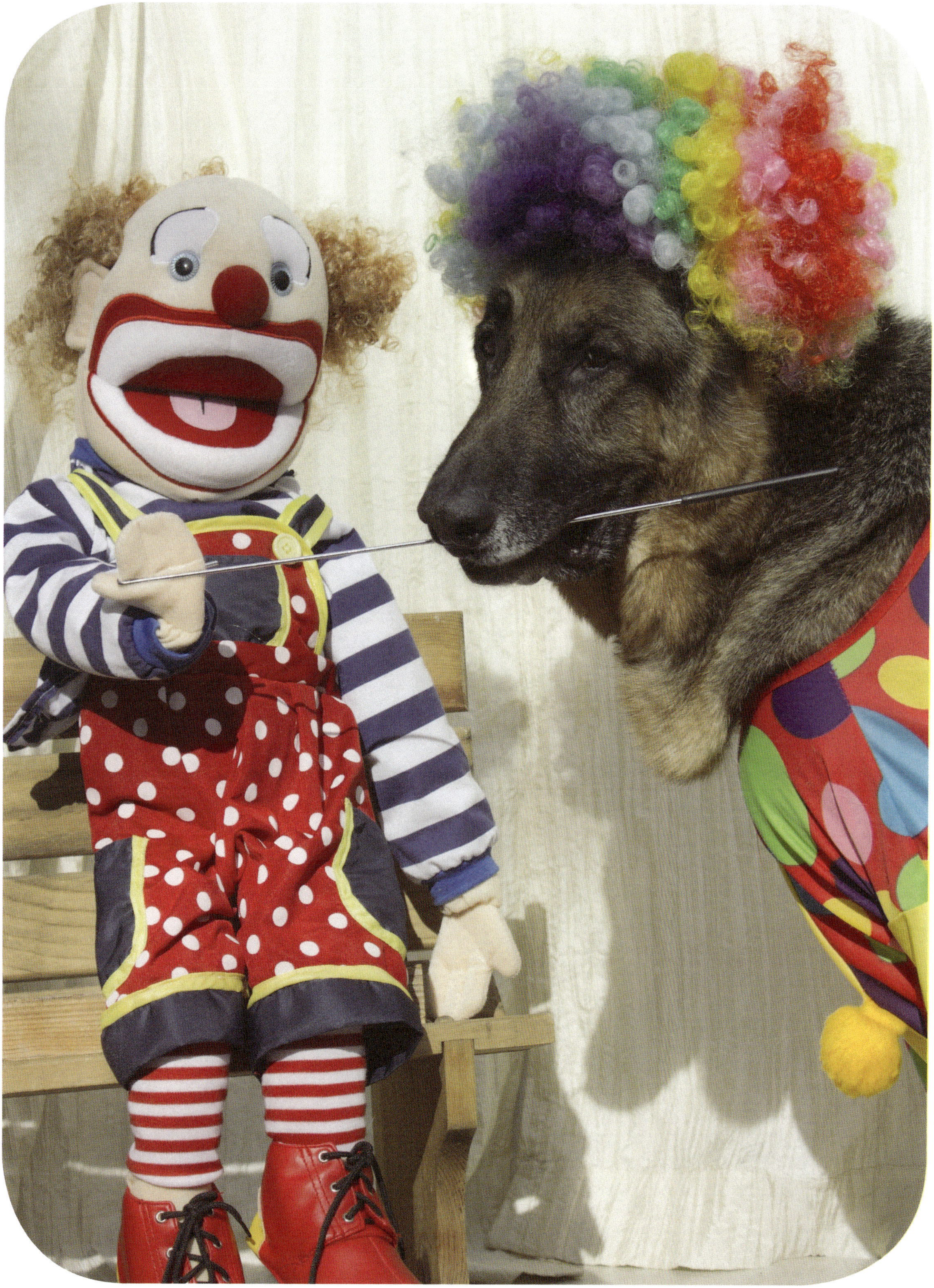

When one of Santa's helpers is needed, Petey is there. He quickly dresses up in his red and white costume and white beard because he likes to help.

Petey says, "It's not so RUFF being a working dog! A dog has to do what a dog has to do."

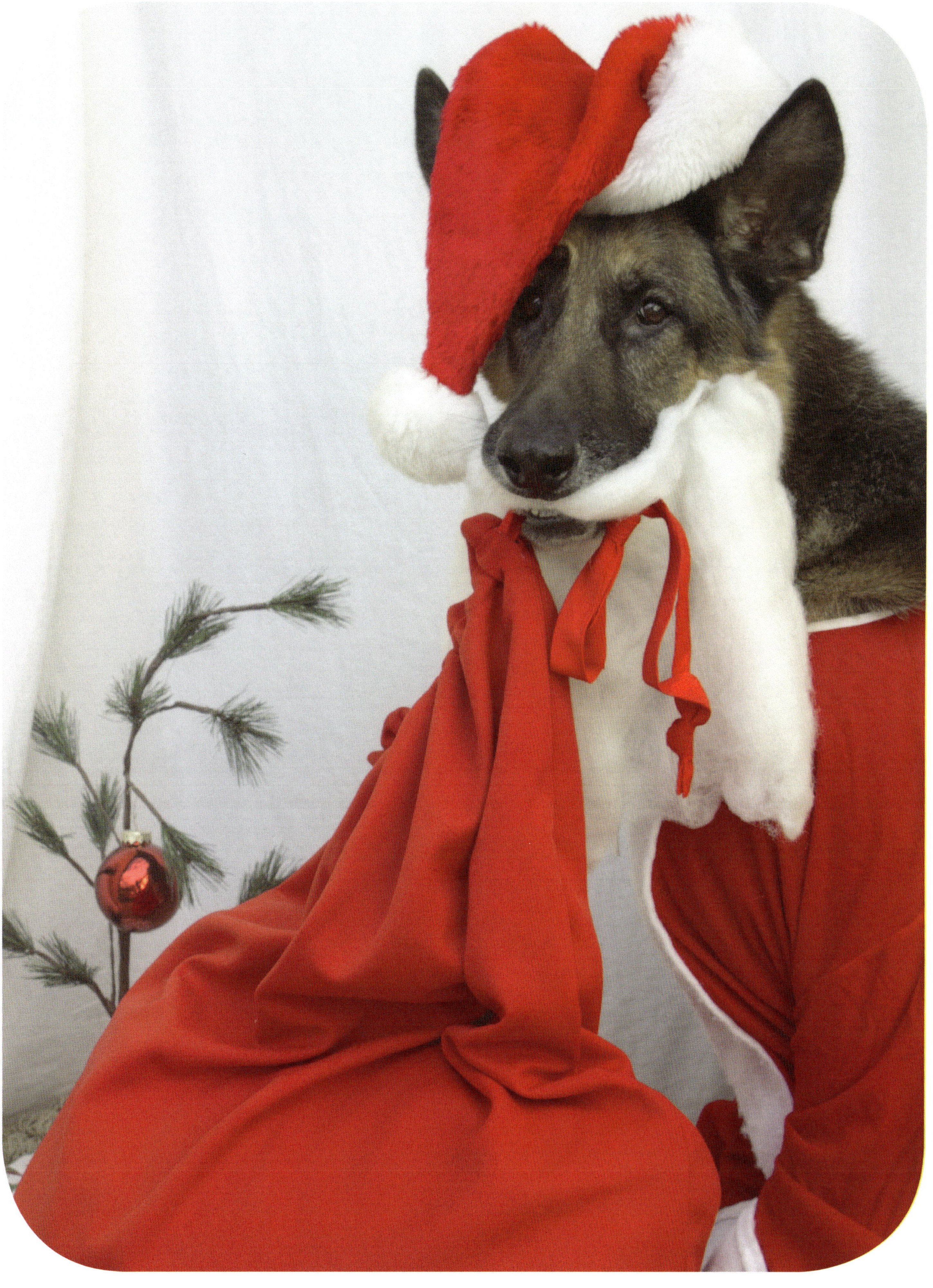

When a superhero is needed to help save the day, Petey is there. He quickly throws on his red cape and mask because he likes to help.

Petey says, "It's not so RUFF being a working dog! A dog has to do what a dog has to do."

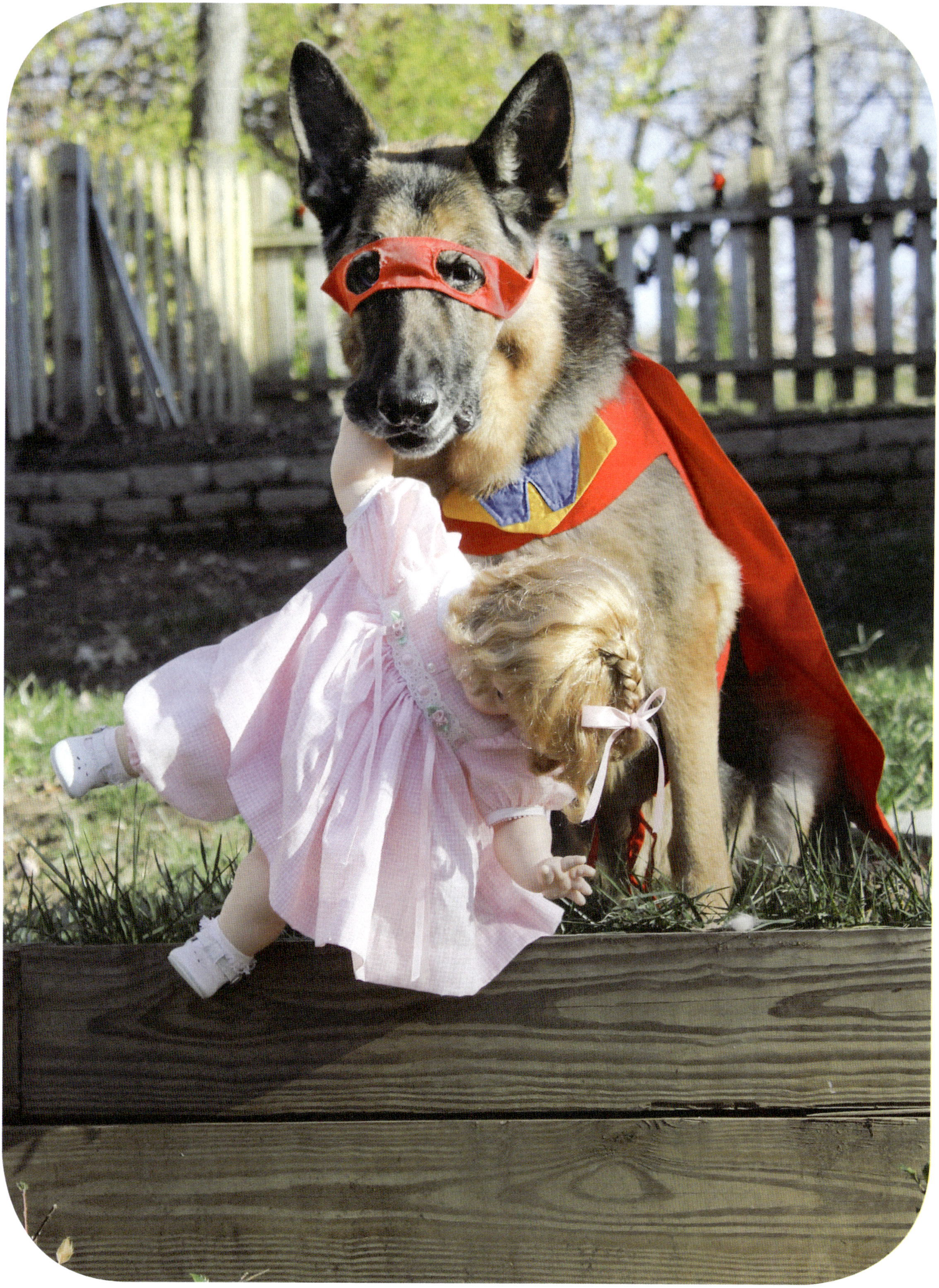

When a service dog is needed to help bring in the groceries, Petey is there. He quickly puts on his harness and badge because he likes to help.

Petey says, "It's not so RUFF being a working dog! A dog has to do what a dog has to do."

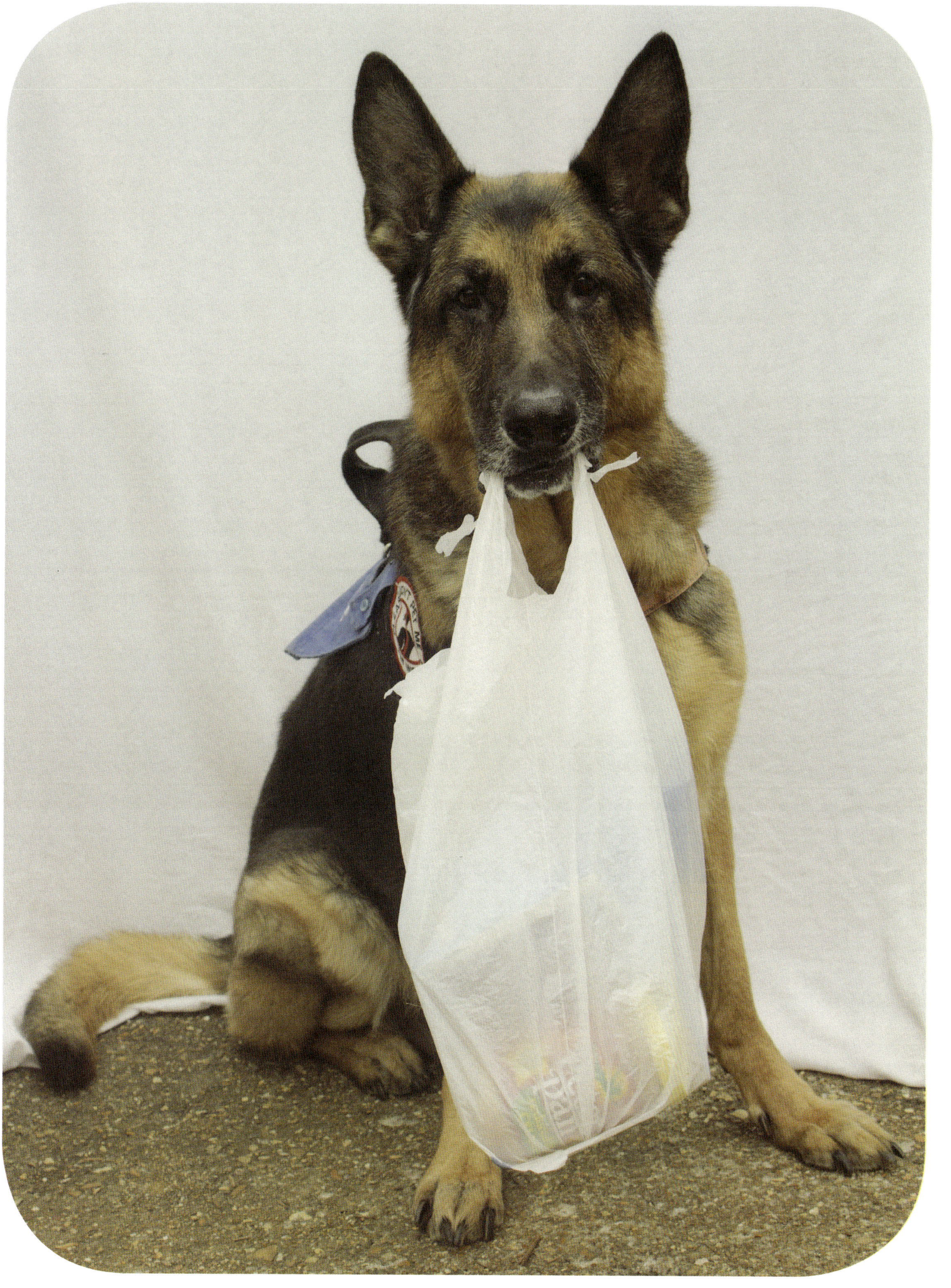

"When no one needs me to help, I get to just be lazy old me. I eagerly wait until I am needed sometime during another day.

Indeed, it's not so RUFF being a working dog! A dog has to do what a dog has to do."

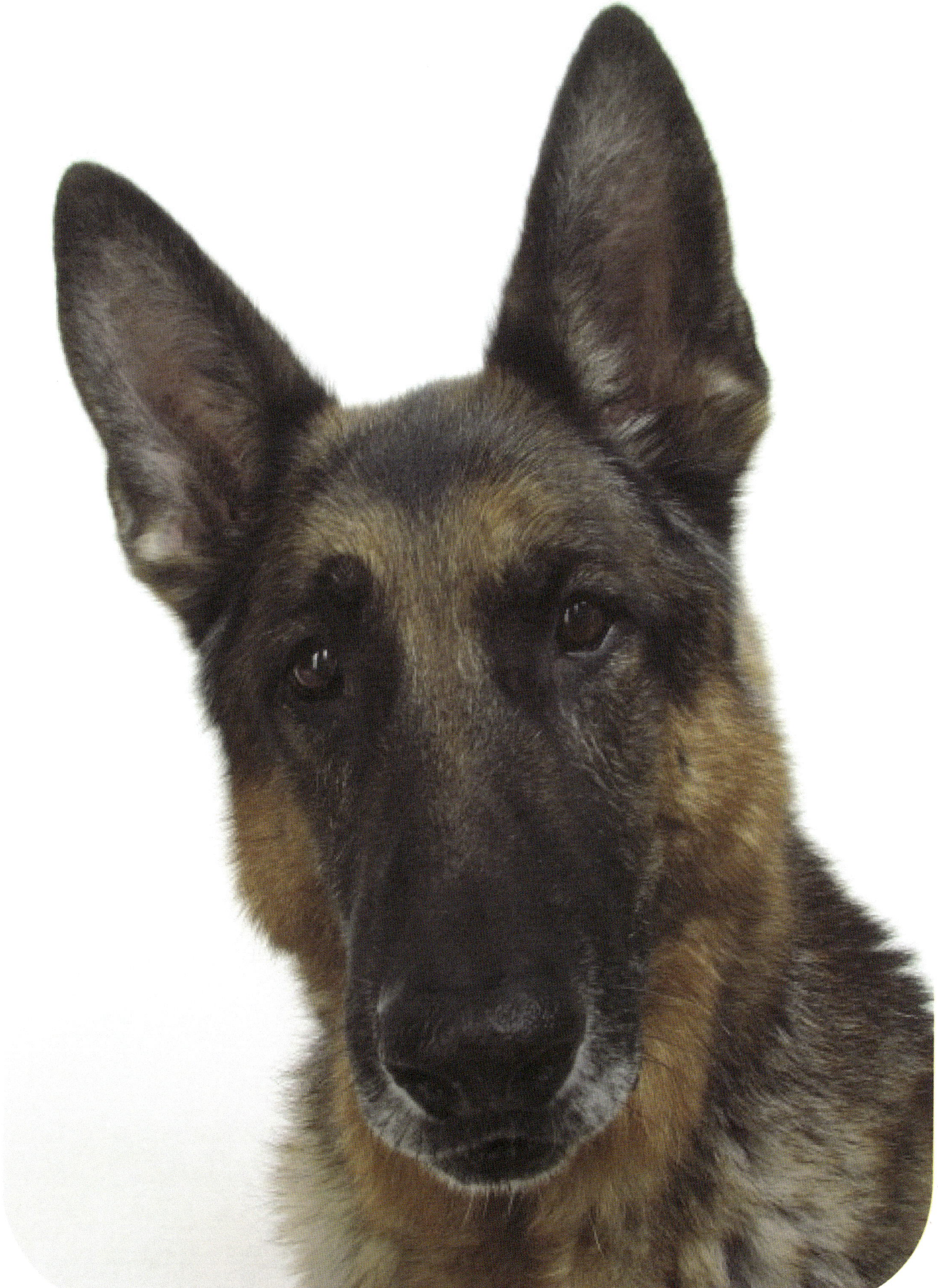

Made in the USA
Charleston, SC
07 October 2014